Contents

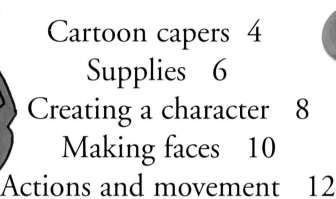

Cartoon capers

A cartoon is a way of drawing people or objects in a simple way. The main features are kept, and often exaggerated, and small details are left out. Animation is all about bringing cartoon characters to life by giving the impression they are moving. Here are some of the different techniques used in making cartoons and animations.

Cartoon strip

This is a series of frames arranged in a sequence to tell a story. Before the finished strip is drawn the frames are roughed out. This is known as a storyboard (see picture above).

Zoetrope

This early form of animation used a cylinder with a series of pictures inside. The cylinder was spun round and the viewer looked at the moving images through a slit at the front.

Art and Craft Skills

Cartoons & Animation

W
FRANKLIN WATTS
LONDON • SYDNEY

First published in 1998 by Franklin Watts
96 Leonard Street, London EC2A 4XD

Paperback edition 2002

Franklin Watts Australia, 56 O'Riordan Street
Alexandria, NSW 2015

© Franklin Watts 1998

Editor: Matthew Parselle
Art director: Robert Walster
Text: Ivan Bulloch, Shona Hynes, Jeffrey Lewis
Illustrators/model-makers: Peter Bull, Ivan Bulloch,
Shona Hynes, Jeffrey Lewis
Front cover illustration: Phil Corbett
Designer: Richard Langford
Photographer: Tony Latham
Cover photography: Steve Shott

A CIP catalogue record for this book
is available from the British Library

ISBN 0 7496 4529 6

Dewey Decimal Classification 741.5

Printed in Belgium

Flick book

Flick books are made from a number of drawings or photographs which show a sequence of movements. The pictures are put together and flicked through with your thumb.

Video

Videos are used by many professionals to make animated films. The video camera is used to film each tiny movement. Completing just a five-minute film can take days, even weeks!

Computer animation

Nowadays, computers are also used by professional animators. Only the first and last stages of a movement need to be drawn and the computer does the rest by filling in the other stages.

Computers can also be used to create characters that look three-dimensional. If you have access to a computer, you may be able to find software for it which allows you to create your own computer characters.

Supplies

The basic items listed below are the main things you will need to do the projects in this book. The shop key shows you where to get them. To get started all you need is a pencil and paper – and probably a rubber!

Shop key

Art supply shop

Craft or DIY shop

Chemist

Stationer's

Supermarket

Toy shop

Paper, card and acetate

1 White paper and coloured card ( ).

2 Acetate (or clear plastic folders) for overlays ( ).

3 Old cardboard boxes for making models ( ).

4 Tracing or greaseproof paper for drawing stages in an animation ( ).

Paints, pens and brushes

5 Water colours are good for painting soft backgrounds ( ).

6 Poster and acrylic paints are good for painting boldly coloured characters to make them stand out from the background ( ).

7 Paintbrushes. Use thick brushes for painting large areas and thin brushes for details ( ).

8 Coloured felt-tip pens and markers make a good, quick alternative to paint ( ).

9 Permanent black pen for drawing outlines on acetate and paper. The ink won't run when you add paint ( ).

Extra equipment

10 Metal ruler for drawing and cutting straight lines ( ).

11 Scissors – use round-ended scissors for safety and sharp ones for cutting thick material like card ( ).

12 Craft knife for cutting straight edges and thick card ( ).

13 Masking tape is useful for marking the position of acetate sheets ( ).

14 PVA glue for sticking large areas ( ).

15 Glue stick for sticking down small areas, like speech bubbles ( ).

16 Plasticine for making models ( ).

17 Metal wire for making the frames for Plasticine models ( ).

18 Modelling tool (or a blunt knife) is good for adding details to Plasticine models ( ).

19 Split pins for keeping parts of cardboard models together yet allowing them to move easily ( ).

20 Pipe cleaners are good for bendy bits on models – like arms, legs and antennae ( ).

21 Bulldog clips are needed to keep the pages of flick books together ( ).

Photography & Film

If you want to record the movements of your characters or models you will need a camera or video camera. You may have these at home or at school. See pages 30-31 for more information on how to use them.

- You can use a camera to photograph each separate stage of an animation, and then use the photos to make a flick book.
- A video camera can be used to make an animated film of your characters.
- A tripod is useful for keeping a camera or video camera stable.

Creating a character

The characters are the most important things in any cartoon. Always try to keep your characters simple. In cartoons and animations you may have to draw characters hundreds of times. If they're easy to draw it will mean less work for you and it will also be easier to make your character look the same all the time.

TIPS

★ When drawing characters it can really help to break them down into circles, boxes, curves and lines to get the basic shape right.
★ Rough out the character in pencil first. Once you're happy with it you can go over the outline in ink and add some colour.

Personality

The first thing you need to decide is your character's personality. Is he or she a hero or a villain, brave or cowardly, friendly or grumpy?

Once you've decided on your character's personality you can change the way he or she looks to suit.

Posture

A character that stoops is usually shy. Someone that stands up tall is probably a confident character.

Clothing

An orderly, efficient character will be neat and tidy, whereas a sloppy and lazy one will be scruffy and dirty.

Shape

The shapes you use to draw your characters can also tell you things about them.

Use curves and circles for a friendly character.

Triangular shapes can look threatening.

Use square shapes for a solid and reliable character.

Making faces

The faces of characters and their expressions tell us a lot about their personality or their mood. To help you draw different expressions, try looking in a mirror and pulling faces. Draw what you see but exaggerate your features.

Faces

A young character may have a big round head and big eyes.

Mean characters have long faces and small, narrow eyes.

Look carefully at the faces of pets when drawing animal faces.

Characters who are tired may have bags under their eyes.

Old people's faces have wrinkles and big jowls by their cheeks.

A nervous character may have wide eyes and an open mouth.

Eyes

The eyes and eyebrows are particularly important in showing the personality or mood of a character. Your character should have a certain expression that is used most of the time. For example, a superhero might usually have a confident expression. Try different eye shapes to see which one fits your character's personality the best.

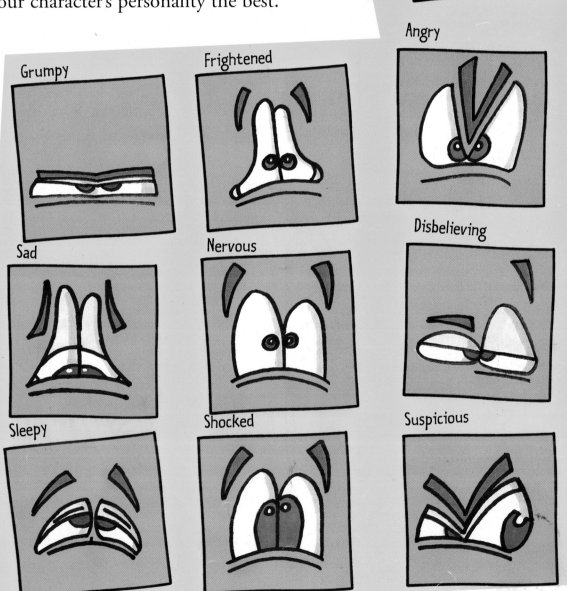

Thoughtful

Angry

Disbelieving

Grumpy

Frightened

Sad

Nervous

Sleepy

Shocked

Suspicious

Actions and movement

To bring your characters to life you'll need to be able to draw them in different poses and doing different things. As with drawing faces, try standing in front of a mirror and pulling various poses at different angles. Memorise them and sketch them down. This will help you when you draw your character doing the same move.

Personality and emotion

A character's personality can be expressed through their movements. Whether they're walking the dog or defusing a bomb, the way they move should fit in with the type of person they are.

Depressed

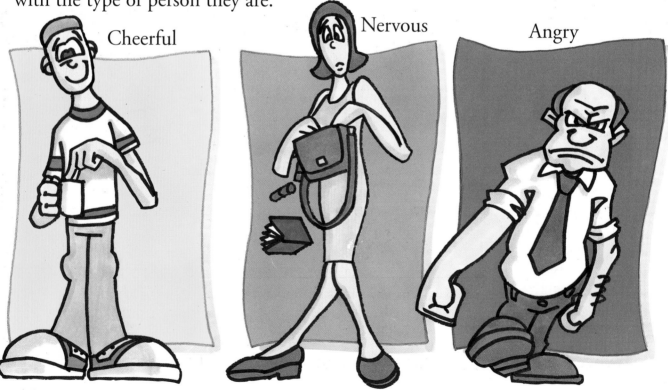

Cheerful

Nervous

Angry

A character's emotion can also be expressed through movement. Below are three examples of the same action (talking on the phone) but with different emotions, and very different body movements!

Normal

Nervous

Angry

Showing movement

There are many simple techniques you can use to emphasise movement. These are some of the most common used in cartoons.

Speed lines

Curved lines

Stars

Curved lines around the corners of an object make it look like it is bouncing or wobbling.

Circling a character's head with stars can be used to show that he or she is dazed or dizzy.

Just a few simple lines give the impression of a character or object moving at pace.

In the background

Once you have created your characters, you will need a setting to place them in. You can keep your backgrounds simple – a horizon line with a few trees will make a good countryside setting. If you want to make them more complicated, you could try cutting out or tracing pictures from magazines or photographs.

Types of background

The type of background you use will depend on where the story is taking place. Here are some ideas for backgrounds for different kinds of story.

A city is a good setting for stories where something extraordinary happens in everyday life, like aliens attacking Earth.

Homes, like cities, are good for stories where strange things happen, like objects coming to life or gremlins creating havoc.

Inside a science laboratory is a good place for a story about a nutty professor trying experiments which go horribly wrong.

Deserts are good settings for adventures about raiding tombs, or where a mad dictator wants to take over the world.

Jungles are ideal settings for stories with animal characters.

Now try this

The shapes you use for the backgrounds can affect the mood of your cartoon.

Sharp, jagged shapes can make a story more frightening.

Round, curvy shapes are good for more peaceful and relaxing scenes.

Use square and rectangular shapes for scenes where everything is solid and well-ordered.

What's the story?

Before you write a storyline for your cartoon strip you'll need a good idea! There are many different types of story – comedy, horror, action, science-fiction... Keep a notebook with you all the time and write down anything funny, sad, quirky or mysterious that happens during the day. Include snippets of conversations, jokes and bits and pieces from magazines and newspapers. These will all be useful when you start writing your story.

TIPS

★ All stories need a strong beginning, middle and end!

★ Watch films and look at other cartoon strips for ideas. But remember, the best ideas are usually original ones!

The script

Once you have a good idea you'll need to write out the story line-by-line. As you're writing, try to think about what the illustrations will be. Our script is about aliens invading the earth.

ALIENS IN THE PARK

A STORY ABOUT JULIE AND BILLY, TWO CHILDREN WHO, WITH THE HELP OF THE INCREDIBLE CAPTAIN R, TRY TO RESCUE A GROUP OF FRIENDLY ALIENS FROM THE CLUTCHES OF THE VILLAINOUS DOCTOR SAGAR AND HIS ARMY OF ROBOTS.

CITY THEY LIV
RUNS NEXT
CYCLES TH
POLICE T
BRIGHT

SCENE 1.
JULIE RUSHES

The storyboard

Now that you have your story, you can start to sketch it out. Break it up into individual frames, show what the illustration will be and write down what is going on in each one. This is known as a storyboard.

JULIE RUSHES INTO HER KITCHEN AND ASKS HER MUM TO TURN ON THE RADIO.

THEY HEAR THAT THREE FLYING SAUCERS ARE APPROACHING THE CITY.

THEY RUSH TO THE WINDOW AND SEE THE SHIPS HEADING FOR THE PARK.

JULIE DECIDES TO RUN TO THE PARK EVEN THOUGH MUM DOESN'T WANT HER TO.

SHE RUNS TO THE FLAT NEXT DOOR WHERE HER FRIEND BILLY IS WATCHING THE NEWS.

SHE DRAGS HIM OFF WITH HER.

The cartoon strip

Now you can begin to draw the finished cartoon strip. Remember that the frames do not all have to be the same size. Try to vary them to give the strip more impact. Some drawings can burst out of the frame, others may not need a frame at all. Below are some devices you can use in your cartoon strip.

Close-ups and angles

You can draw everyday scenes at unusual angles to spice up your cartoon strip.

A close-up is a useful device. It can make a simple event look dramatic and will give the strip more variety.

Try using different perspectives in the strip. You could have a character kicking a football out of the frame.

If a character is in a car, you could try drawing the frame as his view from behind the wheel.

Speech bubbles

Bubbles are nearly always used in cartoon strips to show a character's speech or thoughts. You might find it easier to do these on separate sheets of paper and glue them on when you've finished the picture. Remember to leave plenty of space for the bubbles in each frame.

You can use different types of bubble and lettering to create different effects. For example, big and bold words in jagged bubbles suggest speech which is loud or dramatic.

Cloud-shaped bubbles are usually used to show what a character is thinking.

Zig-zag bubbles can be used for radio, television or computer voices.

19

Flick books

Making and using a flick book is a very simple way to start animating your drawings. Each stage of the animation sequence is drawn onto a separate sheet of paper. All the sheets are then put together in order and flicked through very quickly with your thumb. This gives the impression that your drawings are moving.

You will need

- 10 sheets of stiff paper
- bulldog (or foldback) clip
- pencils and pens or paints
- rough paper

In our flick book, we've used ten stages in the animation sequence. If you want to make a longer sequence, just use more sheets!

1 Think of a simple sequence involving a number of different movements. In our flick book, a boy is ducking to avoid a flying ball, and the expression on his face is changing. Sketch out four stages of the sequence on rough paper to check how it will work.

2 Rough out all the other stages in between these four stages.

Then copy your roughs on to the sheets of stiff paper and paint them.

3 Put all the sheets together in the right order and attach the bulldog clip. Flick through the sheets from the front with your thumb.

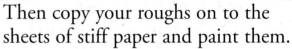

Try making flick books showing different sequences – like an apple being gradually munched away ...

... or someone writing with a pencil.

Moving backgrounds

This is another very simple animation technique. You can use it to give the impression of a character moving across a background. A similar technique is often used in professional animated cartoons.

You will need

* long sheet of paper or card
* pencil
* pen
* paints
* rough paper
* 4 sheets of acetate
* masking tape
* camera (optional)

1 Draw, then paint a background on the long sheet of paper.

Keep it simple so your character will stand out.

2 Draw your character on the rough paper in four different stages of walking or running.

Then lay the acetates on top of them. Trace your drawings on to the acetates with a pen and paint them.

22

3 Place the first acetate at one end of the background. Mark the corners of the acetate with masking tape. This is important because you need to put all the acetates down in the same position. Take a photo of this stage if you are using a camera.

4 Move the background along slightly. Replace the first acetate with the second one and photograph it. Repeat this step for the last two acetates. Carry on, starting with the first acetate again, and continue until you reach the end of the background.

Now try this

Into space
You can use the same technique to create the impression of this rocket flying through space. Make a space background, and paint a rocket on an acetate. Paint two different sized trails on separate pieces of paper. Swap the trails every time you move the background.

You can make a flick book with your photos (see pages 30–31).

Animating objects

You can make 3-D characters from objects that you may have around the house. As with cartoon characters, think about their personality and shape before you start to make them. Try to include a few different parts on their body which are easy to move.

You will need

- old cardboard boxes — large and small
- 3 split pins
- pencil
- stiff card
- PVA glue
- pipe cleaners
- camera
- paints
- (optional)

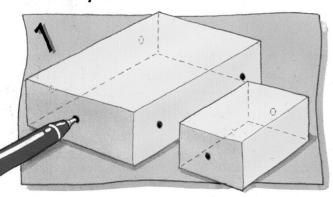

1 Make small holes in a large box and a small box as shown. Paint the boxes and leave them to dry.

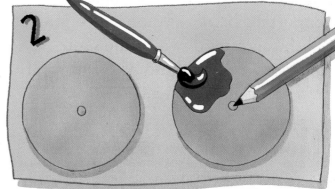

2 Draw and cut out two circles from cardboard and push a hole in each. Paint the circles and leave to dry.

3 Use the split pins to put the two boxes together and to attach the circles.

4 Twist the pipe cleaners and push them into the other holes. Cut a small strip of card. Bend both ends and glue it on. Add a face.

Animating your robot

Try making your robot do simple things, like turn around, twist its head or move its arms.

You can use a camera to record each small movement (see pages 30-31).

Now try this

Fruit folk

You can make a bowl of fruit come to life just by adding plastic shapes bought from a shop. Make a whole family!

Cup final

Make a mad football team from plastic cups, using pipe cleaners for arms. Make a football for them to kick around.

Plasticine faces

Using Plasticine is a great way of creating 3-D characters which can be easily animated. Start by just making a face. You can record movements using photography or video, and make flick books or films of your faces (see pages 30–31). Once you have mastered animating them you can give the faces more personality.

You will need

● Plasticine

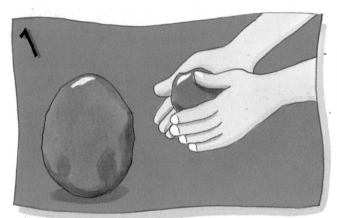

1 Roll some balls of Plasticine with your hands until they are soft. Mould them into shapes with your hands.

2 Make simple faces with eyes, pupils, ears, mouth and a nose. Put the faces on a flat surface.

Animating the face

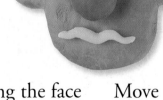

To begin with, just try giving the face some different expressions.

Move the mouth and the pupils around to see how they change.

Now try animating the face in gradual stages. Move the eyes from the left to the right, and the mouth from a grimace into a smile. This makes it look as though the character has seen something he likes.

You can make your character look as though his eyes are following the movement of something, like a plane. Give the face a smile. Move the pupils around the eyes in a circle.

As you move the eyes around, gradually turn the mouth down to give a sad expression. This will make it look like whatever your character was watching has crashed!

Now try this

Once you can do basic animations like those above, you can go on to create funny effects by exaggerating normal movements. For example, you could make your character look as though he's smelling something by stretching his nose, or make his ear grow to give the impression of listening to something in the distance.

Plasticine figures

Once you can make and animate Plasticine faces, you can go on to make whole figures. For Plasticine figures, you'll need to make a wire frame first. This will help to keep the Plasticine in place when you move the different parts of the body.

You will need

- pieces of metal wire
- poster paints
- Plasticine
- modelling tool
- camera (optional)

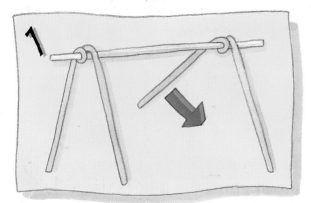

1 Twist two pieces of wire around another piece of wire. This is the body and legs part of the frame.

2 Twist a piece of wire around one end of the body and another piece round the other end for the head and tail.

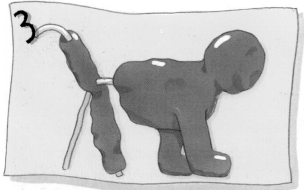

3 Take small pieces of Plasticine and press them around the frame. Add more pieces of Plasticine until you have a basic cat shape.

4 Smooth any joins in the Plasticine. Add a face, ears and paws to your cat. Use more wire to make whiskers. You can paint your cat if you like.

Animating your cat

Put your cat on a clean, steady surface. Lift one paw from each side of your cat off the ground (say the front right paw and the back left). Move your cat along one centimetre.

Put the paws down and lift the other ones up. Continue doing this. Try moving your cat's tail and head as well. You can record each movement on film (see pages 30-31).

Now try this

Try making a dog character for your cat to play with. You can make your dog from Plasticine or you could use sponge. For a sponge dog, make a wire frame in the same way as the cat. Then cut pieces of sponge for the different parts of the body. Push them onto the skeleton, then paint them.

Photography

If you want to record different stages of animation, one of the easiest and cheapest ways of doing it is with a camera. You'll need good lighting. Take your pictures in a bright room and use a flashlight. You'll also need to keep your camera steady – a tripod is ideal for this.

Overhead shots

  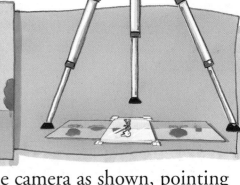

Overhead shots are good for photographing flat objects, like the moving backgrounds (pages 22-23), or things which sit on a flat surface.

Place the camera as shown, pointing straight down at the object to be photographed. Take a picture of each separate stage of the animation.

3-D objects

You can use this technique to shoot 3-D models, like the robot (pages 24-25). Position the camera as shown, at the same height as the model.

Take a photo of your model, then move it slightly and take another photo. Repeat this for each action until you have a complete sequence.

Photo flick book

When you have developed your photos, you can clip them together in order to make a flick book in the same way as you did for the cartoon flick book (see pages 20-21).

Video

For a really professional look, you can use a video camera (if you have one) to film your models. Position it on a tripod in the same way as you would a normal camera.

TIPS

★ Try making a background scene from card for your models to walk around.

★ You can use flexible lamps to help you light the scene. Position them carefully so there are no big shadows on your model.

★ If your camera has a 'single frame' facility, filming is easy. Set the camera to 'single frame' and press record once. Move your model slightly, press record again, and repeat. WARNING: You will have to do this 24 times to make a film which lasts for one second!

★ If your camera does not have a 'single frame' facility you can still film using the record and pause buttons. Press record then pause, before you start. Each time you want to film press pause, count to three quickly, then press pause again. Continue with this until you've finished your film.

Glossary

character (or **personality**) This is what makes people different from each other – the way they move their arms and legs and the way they behave in different situations (pages 8-9, 24-27).

cartoon strip This is a series of single frame drawings arranged in a way to tell a story. You can find them in comic books, magazines and newspapers (pages 16-19).

expressions People show feelings mainly through their faces, using their mouth and eyes. These are called expressions. You can often tell how someone is feeling just by studying the expression on his or her face (pages 10-13).

flick book This is a clever way to make drawings (or photographs) appear to move, like an animated film. Pictures showing a sequence of movements are drawn on separate sheets and held together with a clip. When you flick through the sheets with your thumb, you see the sequence as a moving picture (pages 20-21, 31).

storyboard Cartoon strip and film writers usually map their stories out in a series of boxes. This is known as making a storyboard. The boxes contain rough illustrations which show what will happen in each frame, where characters come into the story, and where the settings change (page 17).

3-D characters Cartoon strip characters are drawn and appear as flat objects on the page. Three-dimensional (3-D) characters, like models or puppets, are solid objects which can be viewed from any angle, like real people or animals (pages 24-29).

video You can use video equipment to make animated films, in the same way that many professional animators do. Instead of just letting the video camera record as normal you set it to 'single frame' record. You then film one frame at a time, moving your character very slightly between each frame. When you play your video back, you will see a moving image (page 31).

Index